If you were here you would feel at home

Michael Favala Goldman

ISBN: 978-81-8253-949-5

First Edition: 2022
Rs. 200/-

Cyberwit.net
HIG 45 Kaushambi Kunj, Kalindipuram
Allahabad - 211011 (U.P.) India
http://www.cyberwit.net
Tel: +(91) 9415091004
E-mail: info@cyberwit.net

Printed at Repro India Limited.

Works by Michael Favala Goldman

POETRY:
Who has time for this?
Small Sovereign
Slow Phoenix
This may sound familiar

CHAPBOOKS:
Balance
Cold Harvest
Unified Light Theory

TRANSLATIONS:
Average Neuroses
Certain Days
Dependency (The Copenhagen Trilogy)
Farming Dreams
Fragments of a Mirror
Inheritance
Liberated
Malvina
New and Selected Poems of Knud Sørensen
Selected Poems of Erik Knudsen
Something to Live up
The Starveling
Stories About Tacit
The Trouble with Happiness
The Water Farm
The Way It Seems

ACKNOWLEDGMENTS:

Gram Clay Pit - Connecticut River Review
Snack - Silkworm
Dawn - Tiny Seed Journal
My thoughtlessness knows no limits - Dead Writers Dance Chapbook

With gratitude to Jette, my partner at home and away

Contents

1

Dawn

And the particles of light from yesterday
who knows where they went.
Did they circle around the earth
or bounce back into space
never to return until the universe
folds back on itself to assist
with reincarnation, coincidence and deja vu?

Regardless I'm still here to invent
myself from yesterday's leftovers.
If I concentrate I can make it seem
like a brand new day, which my eyes
have never seen, my ears never heard.
I'm born from sleep and anything
could happen if I keep waking up.

Morning Tautology

We're standing in the shower more than naked,
one half empty, one half-full, depending
on who you ask.

How can anything be improved when love
is infinite, and how can anything not but degrade,
if not filled and refilled.

We're dripping and I reach for towels,
trying to feel some third thing between or around us,
but all I feel is very me and very you.

I

The way ideas overlap it's unlikely
I will ever have one thought
completely to myself. Boundaries
are made to be breached, must be
perhaps in order to exist: the
paradox of the singular. Seawater
washes in and out the whorls
of a seashell, like sounds and thoughts
in my ears and brain. Everything
is spiraling, and I must follow,
not let my ego hold me, tempt me
into an untenable position.

Whenever possible

Whenever possible broaden.
Let in more of everything
and respond in kind –
more laughter, more outrage.

Now you have the chance
among pirates and angels,
turn mundane into flame
with the flip of a switch.

You're moving along your lifeline
and wham – either its over
or it opens up into a wide valley
which is not a waiting for death.

One degree of separation

Funny how I want to own all kinds of things
yet have trouble putting a finger on
what is truly mine.

When I return from a trip, the things in my house
look at me skeptically. I can't find
a notebook I used to use everyday.

One of my cars won't start, and the dirt path in the woods
I used to walk when I needed to get away
has been paved and a wide line painted down the middle.

If I wake up early my wife kicks me
out of the bedroom and I carry my books
in the dark to a distant quiet pool of light.

My body aches move around day to day
heeding the weather more than me,
craving things that are not recommended.

Meanwhile collective consciousness sloshes
back and forth in my mind. I'm not even differentiated
from the invisible.

Challenge

In this haystack
is a single silver needle.

You don't remember
what a needle looks like?

Like hay, only sharper.
Question is:

Will you find it
or will it find you?

Advice for Self-Promotion

Write under the roots of a tree
for a year

Use the first letters of a poem
to solve the riddle of the most reclusive
stick insect

Attach yourself to a burning page
and blast into the atmosphere

Recite your complete works
while slowly sinking in quicksand

Slide down a Greenland glacier
on a raft of manuscripts into frigid water.

It's not what you do, it's the way you do it.

So explode something, or yourself, but
make sure someone, or a lot of people
are watching.

Crux

S
t
a
y
You are in the crosshairs
t
h
e
r
e

Conclusion

Success is no laughing matter.
How grotesque the worms
eating the pith of my psyche,
the cockroaches scrambling
around the volutes of my imagination.

Whatever I'm turning over
can have snakes or scorpions. I'm thinking
of giving myself permission to leave
things in place, there's so much
I don't need to know.

Future Self

What would you do
if you were me

which you will be
regardless

depending on who
I make myself

out to be right now,
and in all the time

leading up to our meeting
each moment

Don't let me
forget about you

and I won't
let you down.

Aftermath

The last to leave
after the loss,
in no hurry
to remove
from the vacancy
which doesn't feel bad
just tired.

Savoring time
slowing down,
no one misses you,
you are cast
iron, magnetized,
with nothing
in your field, safe
for the time being,
no goal
no obligation, loss
has freed you,
a kind
of victory.

Grief in the Mineral Hills

There's a place near my house
where you can walk on the flat ground
and find yourself surrounded by walls
of striated rock. It's hard to think
how the earth was excavated a little
at a time, long before modern inventions.
It's both a scar and beautiful at
the same time – the silence and echoes,
the pooled water and cattails, the jagged
edges and sheer drops. Rowdy teens
come here to be bad. Once I saw a black
mink scampering along the stepwise wall.
I've been there lots of times but
it always surprises me. It's like a monument,
a void you can walk right in.

Denmark Tour

Drive any long stretch of road
and in the flat landscape see
burial mounds like green breasts
protected by law in the fertile fields,
occasional oak and beech forests
tended for centuries, lichened boulders
of Stone Age settlements, runed
monuments, museums, their artifacts,
relics, ships, braids, jewelry and seeds,
and the present is no longer a larva
dangling on the end of a stem – look
around at the long-boned humans, old
DNA remains alive and well. Life
on equal terms with time. We
surround ourselves with relics:
We are this.

At the Craft Fair

A clear soap
shaped like a hand
with flower petals
to wash my aura

Grime
accumulates
invisibly
How much is this?

Your local correspondent

While residents of Paddington are going
the Kardashian route,
residents of Baker St. are taking things
in a completely different direction,
beautifying their neighborhood as we see
here in the adults and children
clearing, painting & planting together
as long as it lasts, considering the
weather & attention spans, but
how positive to catch people
off their easy chairs interacting
without technology between them,
because Siri is not going to care
for any of us in our convalesence or
old age. But someone has to,
don't they? And now
a word from our sponsor.

Gram Clay Pit

Gram, Denmark

There is at least one place on earth
you can stand
and sink a shovel
into dry, sticky clay
formed 10 million years ago
and the metal blade
penetrates

today's light
enters
where it's been dark
until now

what was
forgotten
is again
in the open

clay
fossils
shells
bones
impossibly old and
suddenly new

They were not waiting
They have nothing
to gain
from our curiosity.

Denmark Sky

What this flat country
cannot offer
in mountains

it makes up for
in clouds

Along the Skjern River

We're walking single file
down an overgrown path
cows and electric fence
on one side
reeds and river
on the other
A long line of hikers.

One points and shouts:
Look, a cloud of birds
Everyone turns
while the starlings' dark
formation like flowing liquid
spreads and gathers
turns toward us
then speeds over the river valley
hundreds of black dots in unison.

We keep walking
Another one says,
It's so amazing
how they move as if
they were one creature.

Copenhagen

I was walking in the city
feeling lonely with people
on the sidewalk being careful
about bicycles and cars and tourists
coming the other way and I smelled
perfume who knows from where
there were some flowers
climbing a trellis on a brick facade
but this was a thick scent the kind
you otherwise never smell except
on a woman up close and I thought
I could go for that for once
be intoxicated and put my life
on hold and surrender to it or
at least to my senses with no
voices in my head at least
not until the next morning and as I
approached an arched passageway
a bridal couple in full regalia
appeared with a photographer and
I nearly stumbled into them
and they didn't notice me at all.

Project

Carrots and a couple of onions,
perhaps chestnuts for the baked squash
for tonight when your sister comes.
While we're staying
in this rental in her town, she's our
laundromat, our source
for bicycles, linens. Meanwhile,
she's our project: How
to change her life without
offending her. We've seen prayer
work, but how quickly? How do we
lure her from her gloom? Does our
secret scheming just make her
feel lonelier? Maybe we should
banish pride and stop trying.
Love her as if she already were
the best version of herself.

Humility

It’s quiet in the early morning
here a couple of miles outside of town
when the day is still muffled
inside walls and comforters. Noise starts
inconspicuously, but still sharper
than anyone wants post-sleep: doors
opening closing, drawers, shoes,
plates, a pen, chairs, silverware. More
doors and car exoskeletons humming, voices,
and the shroud of noise is complete. Whoever
makes the most noise is a demi-god, humble
yourself before Him. Profit now
will have its day, yet again. Silence
never stood a chance.

Take it or leave it

I am referring to my country,
not *the* but *my*, which exists
between the ears of patriots
with real chins. My, or our,
country has no time for weaklings
unable to fathom her
mysterious ways. She's bigger
than all of us, a mother
where the innocent go to die
and the ambitious are granted
eternal life. Show her respect,
thank her for the ground,
or I will show you
a thing or two.

The remark hanging in the air

It’s either a porcupine
or a hunk of butter

Try picking it up
and you’ll find out.

Christiania at 45

There's a wild, medicinal smell
mixing with dampness of the dirt road
as the drizzle falls on Pusher Street
which is not a metaphor, but a place
where photographs are not permitted
and a man will solemnly approach you
if you take out your phone or camera.
There are carts and tables on both sides,
electric multicolored lanterns
hang above like a cheap Rio, clusters
of people ignore the rain, a hand with a knife
slices a dark block of hash for a customer
and I pretend I don't find it unusual, I don't
wonder about making a living in the lawless
quarter, about lives on hold, entrepreneurs,
and just people needing rest. Wc are going
to buy a meal at their little restaurant, think twice
about the tap water, admire the dedication to creating
a crusty dense sourdough to go along with
a thin soup of beans and potatoes. Impressive.
There is definitely something missing from my life.

Christiania is an anarchistic, intentional community founded in 1974 by squatters in a group of abandoned military buildings in Copenhagen. It is largely self-governing.

2

Musica Spei

Sound spirals to silence.

Light spirals to darkness.

We open our silent eyes

to light and are suddenly

full of sweet ideas.

Refuge

I love when covers
    are exactly body temperature
So I'm limitless
    without edges.

Nothing known,
    everything possible.
As long as I don't move
    God can find me.

Naiad

sitting at the spring
teasing out the water

pale fingers
white lace
long hair flowing

to her
this is not work
it's music

while she
makes the element
the element
makes her

and
everything
is wet.

Life before Language

Imagine thought
without words

Image
without description

Interface
with sensation

Immediate

No question

Soundings

Silence is old
and tenacious.

Whenever we stop
making a fuss
silence is still there.

It might be
the most valuable thing
against which all else
is measured
and comes up short.

We do have fun, don't we
revolving around the sun.

The days so astonishingly empty
welcome our thrashing
and our music.

How else are we to learn?

We have to go out
in order to find our way back.

That's right. To that place
at the bottom of us,
at the bottom of everything.

It's peaceful there
and very quiet.

Pinatubo

I don't know anyone who died in the eruption
and I wouldn't blame them for feeling resentful
for being attracted to the place, grand nature
has a pull, a way of almost breaking through
to joy, and then here it goes into chaos or
something that was probably in the back of
a lot of people's minds. Any moment can be
fateful, is actually, and trying to make it more so
might just defeat the purpose. It makes me think
of backing off, like how plants aren't leaping
into the air to get closer to the sun. But it's still sad
whenever something explodes. We can't stop it,
we're too small, so we would do well to take up
battles in proportion to our actual condition.

They can make a huge mess

If there are weasels in your attic you

lie awake wondering what kind of furniture
they are moving across the ceiling

use a stopwatch to time their races and listen
for the arguments over who wins

drive to the nearest animal control and get a trap
put the trap in the yard with two raw eggs
one with a hole poked in it
and be very quiet
especially in the evening

catch one but now animal control is closed
on strike
and don't bother the vet
he wants nothing to do with you

put the cage in your car and drive
to your weekly golf match
stop by some woods on the way
after crossing a body of water

open the trap door and it will look you in the eye

Don't even think of taking it home.

Interface

I can't ask for what I want
but I know what to give you

You can ask for what you want
but you don't know what to give me

I don't ask you what you want
but you tell me anyway

you keep asking me what I want
and I don't know what to tell you

I think you should know by now
You think I still don't know

You think I should know by now
I can't believe you still don't know.

What probably happened

First the snake offered the apple
to Adam
but he wasn't interested –
He was perfectly content
lounging in the garden
naming things.
Why complicate matters.

But Eve knew
their relationship had stalled.
So she took it upon herself
for both their sakes.
For which she has never
been appreciated.

Sad Buddha

So things aren't working out
the way you wish.

Your attempts at controlling
yourself and your
environment are falling short.

So lean in.
Be the sad Buddha,

down to your belly. Maybe someone
will come offer you an orange

Or a rock. The littlest thing
can tip the scales.

Even

Breathe in at birth
        out at death

In between
Who's counting?

Closet

The upper shelf is sweaters and sweatclothes
piled so high it's hard to tell what's there.
On the floor, boxes of old letters, a bowling ball, and
shoes I forget to wear.

Your clothes and shoes are in the other half.
We take turns with the sliding doors.
What will we show up in today?
Will I recognize you?

I've seen you standing in your underwear
staring in as if you might go as you are
but what choice do you have?

You have an eye for detail.
Some days nothing fits.
I'm not that fussy.

What's the problem?

We have everything –
even an isinglass pane.
Neither of us knows where
it came from, though
we have suspicions.

It's the one thing we'd like
to get rid of but
until we know where
it came from we can't
do anything about it.

We keep it
between us.

Sword Swallower

open
up (
you
’re so
accommodating)
no,
it w
on’t
punc
ture
your
stom
ach
just
irri
tate
it re
press
your
gag
so
you don’t
injure yourself
keep it in may-
be I’ll come back
if you call for me.

The Bout

You in your corner
I in mine –

We have to do with each other
but not too much, please.

We rise from our stools
approach the center
keeping the wooden feeling
on our bottoms.

The ref may be our therapist,
or sometimes you, separating us
when we're tangled

sometimes me, prodding us
to re-engage.

The world is watching.

The slack ropes of the arena
mock an escape route.

We have to struggle
as long as there is no winner.

It will be a long match.

Creature of Habit

I've read bodies
remake themselves
every seven years –
skin, ears, eyes.

What have I been doing
all this time
to renew
anything else?

My body is working
harder than me.
Old routines
repeat without trying.

No wonder new eyes
see the same things.
Aches the same places.
I am not innocent.

Situation

After all this time
you're still giving me
not what I want
but what you
want me to have
so you can get it from me.

After all this time
I'm still giving you
not what you want
but what I
want you to have
so I can get it from you.

The expanding universe

Why do you always want something
unattainable? A reputation, a vacation,
a response, a maid. The anticipation
is killing you, as life bubbles up
and drains away, just like that.

You can't have it all, just like the ocean
is never done, it has to keep moving
or life and time would break.
How about making everything
optional? It would add a bit to eternity.

Vacation rental

When I moved my leather bag
the black mold in the corner
was something of a surprise.

The gray spots washed off the bag
with soap and water. Water
is the culprit.

Situated between two lakes
is both scenic and sinking. They say
it was built from a Nazi bunker.

The basement is a bit unusual –
more rooms than necessary,
damp concrete.

When we lie in bed and look
up at an angle we can see black
behind the ceiling edge molding.

We've got to get out of here.

Water is pretty and useful in the right place

Williamsburg, MA, 1874

Our town flooded
like Johnstown
but not as famously
not as many dead

We had our wall
of slurry two stories
high rumble down
taking everything

I welcomed the waves
not because I relish
destruction, I was only
a little afraid

As the water lapped
our foundation, sensing
the new beginnings
to come from

the obliteration, I
wanted everything to be
different. In some ways
it was. Just not enough.

Hydra

It's a logical beast, the easy solution
to our problem, which takes little effort
on my part. It's you who has to change,
grow another head, be the one or many
I always thought you could be. Are you
even trying? You are so slow compared to
my beheadings. I killed you a thousand
times yesterday and you keep returning the same
as far as I can tell. All I see is my own neck branching
with new buds, if only you would take my points of view
as your own, we would be so happy, you and you and you and
you and I and I and I and I and I.

Surprise

There's a void

where neither you
nor I
need
nor give

where anything
can happen

if we resist
making time

serve
us

Don't even put out
your pretty
little toe

3

Reflection in an English village

for Linda

You would see the neighborhood water pump, erect
black iron in its tiny plaza of stone on the street corner,
and notice the handle missing. You would notice
the wildflowers sinking their roots into the softening
triangular rocks topping the lichened stone walls.
You would notice the concrete fill of the basement
kitchen floor, not flat, but practical between the ancient
laid stones. But you wouldn't care. However alive
the present is, the past is more so. So why not
admit it. Why not live with it evident
everywhere, instead of continually buried
or extricated as if it never was. If you were here
you would feel at home.

Spring

It is so generous of the sky
to rain all day
on the seeds I planted.

My lover cried herself to sleep
miserably unable to tell me why.
I didn't know if my touch made it worse.

When I walked out to get the mail
I tipped the umbrella
just a little.

Accommodation

Silence
is so polite.
It says, Please,
you go ahead.
I'll follow you.

Prey

after Suzanne Brøgger

The worst part was not the people
huddled with bundles on the backs
of trucks, the fires behind
or the rubble, the broken bodies,
though it was bad, especially
the children. The worst part
was not the shoes arranged
at the door I went in or the toothpaste
without the cap. The worst part
was the birds singing and the blue sky.
I was not prepared for that.

Tuesday Afternoon

After months away, I take a cart
and enter the supermarket, the one I used
to frequent. I find it
comforting, like any familiar
space, as I know where to find
my repeat purchases all over
this expansive building. And I discover
when I come upon cooking wine half-price
that it's almost like it knew I was coming;
then canned organic beans for ninety-nine cents,
and breadsticks, which they had stopped
carrying a year ago are back
and on sale. The last domestic watermelons
of the year, my favorite pickles, I could go on –
I know exactly what I'm going to make tonight.
My friend is coming over and we have
some catching up to do.

Overrated

Enough of love
I'd prefer some like

I've seen love and its line of
suitcases with surprising contents

I want to show up bare
and not feel exposed

or arrive twisted and be
an interesting sculpture

Love makes the world
go 'round way too fast

Like I can keep up with.

Work

tip p
potential. ing
balanced. acc
d el
e er
s a
i t
a i
r n
r g
e t
t o
t i
a. m
M. p
^ a
^ c
^ t
AGAIN point
hit
START s
mo
me
nt rs

te
at
sh

Not doing

At the end of the lawn
stands a tall fir
which doesn't rush
into anything
I'm sure it's been
right there
fifty years
or more
growing
imperceptibly
(who has time to watch?)
to well over a hundred feet tall
making cones and needles.

Everything comes to it:
sunshine, pollinators,
water, soil, air – just the basics
and when the big dragonflies
come sweeping
around sundown
the tree doesn't swat
at them
maybe it doesn't even
marvel
just considers them
as any birds
yet something else
giving it purpose.

Unfathomable

Nature
is a study in
approaching infinity

Creeping beetles
grandfather trees
ocean swells

All the same fabric
stretched infinitely thin and deep
across the surface of the planet

Try and replicate it –
you cannot succeed
with rational thinking.

Shock

When you walk in and
there's someone there

or no one there

and you're in the jaws
of the overwhelming

what's the point then of feeling

You're numb

Better to take it in gradually
over the rest of your life

You have plenty of time.

To one who is trying

Considering

the circumstances

taking

everything into account

not only is it obvious

you are doing

your very best

you are also

absolutely

being yourself

better

than anyone else.

My thoughtlessness knows no limits

I continually place scraps
and pocket junk on the dresser
though my wife says
I should not do this.

I go out to the woodshed
and the garden
in my office pants
(just to do a little bit!)

I don't wait up
for my kids to come home

And this morning I swept up
tissues that missed the waste basket
with my new Selected Poems
of William Carlos Williams.

Snack

I don't know how many people noticed
when she came up to me in the cafeteria
and handed me a little box which
I thought might have contained a piece
of veggie pie, and said, "This is a Christmas present,"
and when I took it with a polite thank you,
she planted her lips right on mine
with a gentle suction and held them
there and held me and didn't let go
and I was both enjoying and evaluating,
my body was going back and forth
between right and wrong until finally
I was able to back my lips out and
then you returned – from the ladies room
or getting napkins?– and we ended our
embrace and I turned to you with my
slightly crumpled box, handed it
to you saying, "It's a little snack,"
and as we walked out you lifted the lid
and picked out a chunk of beet, popped it
into your mouth, since you know
they're not my favorite.

Last chance

I think this is just
a little problem
that I have plenty of time
to work it out

Actually
my hair is on fire
and I am downplaying
my need for water

I'm blinded
by lesser needs
while sinking in the quicksand
of my hourglass.

And then he put his finger in the soft candle wax and spread it on the window screen

Out in the middle of our side lawn
lies a block of emmenthal and a
sharp knife. – Is it bait? We had a bear,
a large black one, amble through right at
this spot last week on his thick
shaggy legs, doing the mambo.
The cheese was probably courtesy
of Mary's two-year-old, who's visiting.
Makes you wonder how his mind works,
how or when logic is built up
in a person's mind, reining in limits
of possibility, so as not to inconvenience
others. I'm the one who does the lawn,
so I'll deal with it. It's too quiet.
Someone go check on that kid.

Sixth Sense

My wife makes a drawing motion at me
from across the room which means
to take out drawing supplies
because the little kid is getting restless
and we need a diversion here
at the city hall so she can finish
her business with the department. Children
adore her because she senses their
needs in advance, before they reach
critical mass and inconveniently explode.
I'm a useful servant, carrying toys.
It's all about the kids, keeping them
content, like regulating weather.
I do what she says, and soon he's
doodling away, one more small rescue
in the obstacle course of the day.

Beachcomber

Pia is writing a novel.

She goes down to the ocean and watches the sea foam
skimming like ghost feet over the sand.

Words come blowing through her.
Her ears are howling with salt spray and stories.

Like a sieve she catches what she can use.

Through the dune grass and heather she returns to her cabin
and sifts through what is now hers.

Wheelbarrow

Borne across the field of day, bouncing
                        on ruts, loading and un-
                        loading above a rotating
                                            axis   the
                                          planet   tipping
                                          time   to a standstill

Osmosis

In the end, things even out.
It's all about concentration.
What's inside has to move
outside and vice versa.

Thunder, knowledge –
homeostasis
may be the ultimate
the unachievable.

God is osmosis,
the irresistible
boring agent
of change.

The finch

It's sundown and the goldfinch
swoops by, undulating yellow
on the waves of the air, chirping
a bright tune to her lover,
"My sunflower, my sunflower," she
repeats again and again, alighting
on his frilled head, singing as she twirls
on his mane and pecks
at his face, eating with delight
the kernels in the black fertile drops,
while dozens fall to the earth
and he grows more and more blind,
more and more blank,
and she sings his praises for now
and for the future, they will always be
together in the summer
together in the dwindling light.

I meet you in a place which does not exist

We exist
and as we meet
we disappear
and the meeting disappears
as we keep meeting

What exists is the memory
of that place
which does not exist
except in memory
and in meeting

The Swallows at Eagle Lake

This is the time for which the swallows have been waiting
when the sun on its way down has just touched
the treeline across the water, and they come
swooping, flapping, swirling, slashing
the air above the greengold reeds
they chirp and dart, streamlined silhouettes
feasting before the closing curtain of dark.

As the sun dips below the trees we get up
from our bench and walk through clouds
of tiny insects smaller than increments
of time and wonder how many
it must take to fill the life
of even one swallow
how many swoops, how much delight
the hunger is barely about eating
it's about flight and the turning earth.

www.ingramcontent.com/pod-product-compliance
Lightning Source LLC
LaVergne TN
LVHW040952150826
845672LV00002B/654

* 9 7 8 8 1 8 2 5 3 9 4 9 5 *